This book is to be returned on or before
the last date stamped below.

Poetry by Stewart Conn

Thunder in the Air (Akros, 1967)
The Chinese Tower (Macdonald, 1967)
Stoats in the Sunlight (Hutchinson, 1968)
An Ear to the Ground (Hutchinson, 1972)
Under the Ice (Hutchinson, 1978)
In the Kibble Palace: new & selected poems (Bloodaxe Books, 1987)
The Luncheon of the Boating Party (Bloodaxe Books, 1992)
At the Aviary (Snailpress, Cape Town, 1995)
In the Blood (Bloodaxe Books, 1995)

STEWART CONN

In the Blood

BLOODAXE BOOKS

ISBN: 1 85224 329 5

First published 1995 by
Bloodaxe Books Ltd,
P.O. Box 1SN,
Newcastle upon Tyne NE99 1SN.

Bloodaxe Books Ltd acknowledges
the financial assistance of Northern Arts.

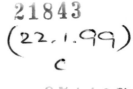

Cover printing by J. Thomson Colour Printers Ltd, Glasgow.

Printed in Great Britain by
Cromwell Press Ltd, Broughton Gifford, Melksham, Wiltshire.

to Judy

Acknowledgements

Acknowledgements are due to the editors of the following publications in which some of these poems first appeared: *Cencrastus, Chapman, The Dark Horse, Edinburgh Review, Gairfish, Headlock, The Independent, Klaonica: poems for Bosnia* (Bloodaxe Books/*The Independent*, 1993), *Lines Review, London Magazine, New Writing Scotland, Orte* (Switzerland),*The Scotsman, The Southern Review* (USA), *Spectator, Spectrum, Stand, The Stony Thursday Book/Cuaderno de Madrid, Under Cover* (Mainstream, 1993), *Verse* and *West Coast Magazine*.

The Upper Clyde poems are from a sequence originally commissioned by the *Glasgow Herald* which appeared, with photographs by Edward Jones, as a *Weekender* feature on 3 December 1994. 'Strangers in the Night' was commissioned for *Fallen Angels* by Jack Vettriano and W. Gordon Smith (Pavilion Books, 1994) and first read at the anthology's launch in Edinburgh City Art Centre.

The cover painting, *Hinterland* by Barbara Rae (5′6″ x 6′6″, acrylic collage on canvas, 1994), is reproduced by kind permission of the artist.

Contents

III.

I

Kilmarnock Edition

Not *that* one but a pictorial volume
presented by Kilmarnock Burns Club, won
as a prize for recitation, and taken

to a supper I was arm-twisted into
by my English teacher;
then erased from my mind, till a quarter

of a century later, moving house,
my wife, thumbing through it, found
a rash of asterisks obscuring *To a Mouse*

and in the margin, directions to accompany
that mid-50s rendering: 'Start softly':
Wee sleekit, cowrin', timorous beastie...

'Hand on chest': *Oh what a panic's in thy breastie!*
Then 'pensively': *I'm truly sorry man's dominion...*
The audience mesmerised no doubt, as I mimed

the *cruel coulter*, gave the *daimen icker* laldie.
But behind self-mockery, I'm conscious
of the duality that revels in revealing

feet of clay, yet sups up sentimentality,
and hope I toed a line mid-way,
purveying an underlying genuineness

of feeling. In our world of violence, greed
and posturing, never greater need
for restating his criterion of goodness:

whatever mitigates the woes
or increases the happiness of others.
Declared hand on chest, or otherwise.

Ayrshire Coast

Sandy links and raised beaches...made Ayrshire a
prime resort for Victorian and later pleasure-seekers.
RIAS GUIDE: 'Ayrshire & Arran'

West Kilbride, Gailes, Barassie, Troon,
Prestwick, Bellisle and points between:
so the links courses of our schooldays
unfold like an apron of green baize
brooched by gorse and dune, down Ayrshire's
coastline. This year's Masters, watched
in comfort by satellite, contrasts
with that monochrome age, when first prize

in the *Daily Mail* Tournament (all of £250)
went to Dai Rees for 'four sturdy rounds';
his autograph, alongside Henry Cotton's neat
hand, a reminder of what we were desperate
to emulate – only to learn in life how rather
than the dream parabola adolescence yearns for
(golf's equivalent of the perfect iambic pentameter)
the ball dips and veers through unsupporting air.

Enforced holidays on Troon beach made the most
of ice-cream vans enveloped in sea-mist;
chittery-bites seized on; female underwear
seen surreptitiously, as one-piece swimsuits
were discarded – paleness of thigh and breast
projecting neither guilt nor embarrassment,
which in those days seemed not carnal, or remote,
but simultaneously peerless and innocent.

A different proposition when we danced
a decade later, to Harry Margolyes
and his Band, at Ayr's Italianate Pavilion
Ballroom; and on the prom on autumn
evenings, walking arm in arm, glimpsed
through fumbled skeins of blonde or auburn,
lighthouses blinking from afar; then
to return, our numb cheeks flecked with brine.

*

Despite erosion, the coastline scarcely
changed. Except, where we believed the breakers
would always surge purely, squalor has taken over;
successive tides jettisoning scum and debris.
You can drive on south toward Heads of Ayr,
gaze averted to Arran and its Sleeping Warrior.
But hard to stomach, the beaches where we sat
unfit for a European health certificate.

A history not short on brutalities:
where Alexander routed Haakon's invaders –
Nardinis wicker-chairs and brash *torchères*;
unmarked graves, and the occasional stone
where fleeing Covenanters were hacked down;
while in Dunure's black-vaulted dungeon
for the Commendator of Crossraguel's
basting, Cassilis 'spared not flaming oil'.

Confidently claimed Scotland's microcosm,
Arran preserves its own social schism:
the hotels in Brodick, Lamlash and Whiting Bay
part of a douce but rigid hierarchy;
coach-parties welcomed by some, not others;
guest-houses girt for the Glasgow Fair
when the crowds would mill, and glutted gulls
followed the churning of great paddle-wheels.

Even in this haven, shades of *timor mortis*:
of the glowing Academy girls we rowed,
one succumbing early to sclerosis;
others performing the offices, for the dead.
Amongst summer's specialties meanwhile
persists the democracy of the bicycle;
with rucksacked cohorts setting out to tackle
the rock-chimney of Glen Sannox, and Goat Fell.

*

The Season ending, B & B signs come down;
the daily ritual of the sheets ceases;
skimpy guest-towels are returned
to store. Arcades of fruit-machines
empty. Vacated caravan sites
reveal their own *mal du pays*.
More grave the varieties of silence,
year round, where diverse activities

once were: boat-building in harbours
made derelict; Ardeer's work-force
hit by the rigours of redundancy.
To freewheel down (or up) the Electric Brae
an ideal metaphor for the economy;
Culzean's castellations, provenance
of the rich; and on the skyline, defunct
Ailsa Craig, Cuchulain's curling-stone.

In a county of milk-yielding heifers,
creameries producing ersatz cheeses;
lace curtains still gracing Newmilns
and Darvel – but their heyday undone
by cheap labour from Japan. Pit closures,
dignity once attained at the coalface;
rails rusting from Doon to Dalmellington:
Cockburn's 'last place in Ayrshire where

with a good deal of primitive manufacture,
rural simplicity and contentment linger' –
its Age of Iron having come and gone...
Whisky aside, the one sacrosanct industry
centres on Alloway. Burns statues scan
a World which while paying lip-service,
reveals less and less his philosophy
of brotherhood, than Man's inhumanity to Man.

Early Days

Connections

Changing trains at Glasgow Central *en route*
for a poetry workshop in Kilmarnock I visit
the bookstall which has, needless to say, none
of my volumes on display. Nor any sign
on the departures board of my connection,
I'm so early. Eventually it appears:
objective reality restored, at least. Soon
the old litany: Dunlop, Stewarton, Kilmaurs...

As my fellow-travellers, secure in their
identitics or otherwise, journey on
towards Sanquhar, Carlisle, my reception
counters expectation: a strummed guitar,
the car in a tarmacked space where rails once were,
set in cobbles, to ease the dray-horses' burden.
To an unaccustomed music, and hyacinths in bloom,
the decades dissolve, and we coast into town.

School motto

Among my memories
a smell of modelling clay
(this before coloured plasticine)

rows of Mickey Mouse
gas-masks (placing me
in the early 40s)

and school caps, regularly
floating like rowan berries
down the Kilmarnock water.

Our infants mistress
Annie C. MacLarty FEIS
took us to her ample bosom

before handing us over
to Davy Gordon, who ruled
with a rod of iron.

In senior school
we were further matured
by two breakdowns and a suicide.

Later our French master
went into mourning, when
a colleague's son got only

a third at Aberdeen.
By then, we others had gone
our own way: unshriven,

but trying (some of us)
to *do justly, love mercy,*
and walk humbly.

New Farm Loch

We skated here after school,
breath visible in the frosty air,
chestnuts sizzling, the ice
ringing. Or played football,

blazers for goals, Tom Campbell
ghosting down the wing,
others less skilled
picked as a cock or a hen.

Drained long since,
the loch's declivity
holds a housing estate.
Yet I sense presences

blowing on their fingers
as if all these years later
my schooldays were pursuing me
through acres of trees

no longer there. The one
tangible reminder a hole
in my left knee, where
the heel of a skate sank in.

Arm's reach

Of moments treasured:
having scaled the tree,
ripe pears gathered
unbruised. Some
peeled and preserved
in syrup. The remainder
each year, painstakingly
stored in paper and straw.
The tubbed windfall, mush
for wasps. These days, even
could I climb to the top,
I'd most likely find
the branch and its fruit
just out of arm's reach.

Mirror image

Evening drawing in, I revisit old
haunts: the Burns monument, smaller
than I recall; St Marnock's, its trees squat
as ever; and facing the Dick Institute
the sandstone Academy, dominant on its hill.

Over a couple of pints in the Goldberry
I'm told I don't sound like I'm really
from Killie, the intervening years
having added an overlay. But things seem
to go smoothly. So that by the time

I reach the station I'm confident
I could pass for local. Till reflected
in the waiting-room window, I see
a familiar figure carrying a plastic
bag emblazoned '*Ayrshire and the Burns country*'.

Spring

Ayrshire is breaking into leaf, you say,
then convey in detail sound and scenery,
fresh limes emerging, a grasshopper warbler's
whirring song. It makes me think of Daphne
fleeing Apollo, and her father's answer
to her prayer: leaves sprouting from her hair
and hands, bark shielding her quivering body.
The one a timely metaphor for the other:
the dew, escaping its lover's ardour,
leaving nothing but verdure, where
a moment earlier, it sparkled purely.
You'll be telling me next how lovers lie
languid under every laurel tree; Aurora
filling the air from Girvan to Dunure;
Arran's outline clear, across a wine-dark sea.

White Tulips

Over the years, now decades, memories sporadically
surface for no seeming reason: among them one
of a classmate's sister who, playing one day
at the Creamery, must have tripped and fallen in.
I still shudder involuntarily, at the pain
encountered, the scalding of her skin; and can
but pray her engulfing was mercifully speedy.

As I sit in the garden this fragrant May afternoon
she comes to mind, incongruous light-years away.
First there's the shiver that coursed through us,
who at that age thought ourselves scatheless.
Only after this, do I consciously take in
these tulips beside me, their ghostly whiteness
grown suddenly diaphanous in the light breeze.

Troon Revisited

(for Stuart Paterson)

Never a swimmer, my dominant memory
of Troon beach is of a toe half-severed
by broken glass, the painful hirple
to the house. At this remove even,
I tread gingerly. Constants: the spire
of St Meddan's, Marr's copper dome;
tankers that seem moored since last time.

Less propitious: peeling frontages,
grimy dunes netted against erosion,
engendering insecurity, gentility
going to seed. Sensing an epoch gone,
I recall the zigzag from tee to green
when in our heyday we tackled Fullarton,
then cycled to savour Togs's famed ice-cream.

Concession too, of disillusion within
a personal littoral. The harbour shrunken,
the Ballast Bank less precipitous –
accomplices to further self-perception:
as with a mountain cairn, its attainment
once a measure of achievement, found
to be no more than knee-high, Lilliputian.

The town itself, once 'one of Ayrshire's
leading ports', reverting more and more
to how we saw it: breaking-up yard
for the elderly, where the retired
sit under glass, among potted geraniums,
the air growing acrid as they doze
or drily scrutinise their stocks and shares.

Along the front, those solid Victorian
villas, double-glazed which in our day
were heavy-curtained, but still draughty;
and in a crescent below the station,
behind blowsy roses and laden trellises,
the curvaciously bow-windowed bungalow
we as schoolboys nicknamed *Marilyn Monroe*.

Countering this, the mock 15th century
rigour of Our Lady of the Assumption,
in the shadow of whose buttressed tower
worshippers briefly shiver. I look up, to see
the crocketed finery of its timber spire –
and far beyond, against an azure sky,
white jet-trails crossing, a perfect saltire.

Terra Firma

The church of which my father was minister
lowered over my boyhood, its front elevation
imprinted on the retina; an endowed carillon
spendthrift expenditure of a sum more
practical if put towards the maintenance
of rotting roof timbers and friable sandstone.
Although latterly dwarfed by the Police Station
and Sheriff Court opposite, an architectural
survey recently lauded its structure
from hood-moulded main door to battlemented tower,
not to mention *the pulpit's fine expression*
of the crescendo of the Gothic revival...

We'd never have guessed (far less cared)
when as children we fidgeted on hard pews,
that those encompassing walls in future years
would be praised as *scholarly perpendicular* –
a paradox sharpened by the then snobbery
of the town's more class-conscious clergy
one of whom murmured, after his ordination,
'Of course St Marnock's isn't on the map, Conn'.
Throughout his calling, in ways I was then
too young to comprehend, he remained his own man:
voicing concern for single mothers, whom
the Kirk's committees saw as 'fallen women';

and believing an unfashionable ecumenicalism
the way to enlightenment, debating at Coodham
and courting the Kilmarnock Standard's abuse
by counting among his friends, RC priests.
As through a glass darkly, I have come
to a more comprehending admiration
for the industry and integrity
he must have channelled into his ministry –
rather than any inheriting of beliefs: partly
because he never exerted pressure
but permitted me to go my own way,
doubtless praying it would not be to purgatory.

Those moments uppermost, at a lifetime's remove,
of austere ritual, redeemed by love
under the lights of the Christmas tree;
and at harvest festivals, ripe sheaves
round the walls of the shadowy vestibule,
fruit heaped before the communion-table,
then the delivery of flowers and vegetables
by the Bible Class: a child's view of the tangible
manifestations of others' belief in Divinity,
not the tenets sustaining it. Today
the building stands, like a preserved dragon –
forbidding still, but no longer breathing flame.

Castles

Loudoun little more than a shell,
which in its day bore the title
'Windsor of the north'. At Dundonald, yowes
graze in a king's resting-place.

With groined vault, blocks of ashlar,
Craigie more than a match for
any, till its tower-house abandoned
by the Wallaces, and ruined.

Made watter-ticht wi diligence
at a michtie princess's expense
Dean's minstrel gallery a reminder
of the Boyds' puissance and grandeur.

Colourful still, their forays;
names given to school houses –
Loudoun, Dundonald, Craigie, Dean:
red, blue, yellow, green.

Peace and Plenty

On autumn Saturdays we'd cycle
to Caprington Estate with its great
chestnut trees: the lawns littered,
each spiky bur split on impact,
ripeness preserved intact.

Pockets filled, we hurled up sticks
to dislodge what more we could –
eager to get at the Upper Crust
with their stately homes and shiny
Daimlers, the only way we knew.

Ingrained, a callow awareness
of revolutionary days, eggs thrown
at carriages, *aristos* done down.
Their ruined mansions seen later
as bombastic parodies of what they were;

our middle-classness an encumbrance
rather than aligning us
with miners' families
or those in the neat cottages
known as Peace and Plenty,

harking back to an age
presaging a New Dawn.
Hard to take, the fruits
of promise not justice
but a polarisation such

as we've seen; retributive
Government seeking scapegoats
among Society's weakest;
stooping to enlist folk-myth
in ways we never dreamt of.

Depths

Wakened in the small hours
by a dull clang (too early
for the binmen) I find
sleep dispelled, by sounds
of a different kind.

Buckets are being filled
at the head of the byre:
accompanying the splash
of water, a rhythmic swish
of hard bristle, down the gutter.

Then something else
I do not want to hear;
a series of plaintive squeals,
accompanied by others
less high-pitched yet sharper.

Alone in a chill dawn,
I listen to a muscovy cat tear
with her claws at the sliding door
as in the great tub, I hold down
the sack in which her kittens drown.

Country Dance

Before the advent of the combine
the Big Mill would lumber from farm
to farm, spouting steam and flame:
stooks extending to the horizon
and beyond, weathered by sun or rain.

Intricate as a dance, was the tying
of the sheaves, on the ground
or against one thigh, to a communal
rhythm; then their hoisting
in the stackyard, forks flashing;

and as though riding on air,
the man on top, under steady
bombardment, circling and weaving,
gold ramparts rising round him
to a music compelling as any eightsome.

Map of Coningham

being the North Part of *Aire Shire*, **by Thos. Kitchin** (1718–84)

(for Gerry Cambridge)

This 18th century 'map of Coningham',
part-tinted, unobtrusively fits in
with our kitchen decor, its simplicity
in keeping with earlier watercolour days:
Kilmarnock central to its intimate universe,
as so it seemed; in identical type-face,
Craigy and *Eglintoun*; and like a wire
slicing cheese, one road aslant the Shire.

In my inner ear those years remain encased –
precise as birdsong, their crisp cadences.
Minimal brushstrokes meanwhile, under glass,
summon a parallel vision of the past:
a world of distinctive cattle, white and brown,
antique machinery, loads that are horse-drawn;
and industrious generations, who belong
to the soil as it, for a spell, belonged to them.

A rurality stoutly asserted, when at school
we resisted those determined to rinse
Scots from our mouths. Ours too a dual role,
would-be city slickers, lads about town
eager to flaunt, when following Killie,
the vocables of our industrial milieu;
till a visiting fan with fouler glottals
roared 'Get tore in at thae country yokels!'

Distance not simply framed fastidiously,
but scaled in accord with 'English miles';
degrees longitude, anachronistically
west not from Greenwich but from Edinburgh
whose inhabitants, wholly oblivious
of our lives' minutiae, would have been
shocked at the vehemence of our disdain
for the noses they supposedly looked down.

This later conceded as anti-snobbery,
itself supplementing a dichotomy
of urban and rural selves – identity
so split, as to feel an outsider either way;
remaining at heart uncertain if I stem
from town or country; born and bred a son
of the manse, yet experience most intense
in that half moon's cropped and tilled expanse:

few nightmares worse than a stallion
splintering stable doors, or hell more real
than the limepit into which a horse
and cart were sucked, when I was small.
So that despite gulfs of time and space,
a world remote but for a rectangle
on a wall, I still think of my shoes
holding a sprinkling of rich Ayrshire soil.

The American Girl

I recall the low ceilings; velour curtains,
oppressively drawn; silver cups turned
into lamps; and on the parlour wall, a framed
print I assumed was my great-uncle, before
he was lamed: whip held high, hands firm
on the reins; the mare's nostrils flared,
white of her eye protruding; the shafts
so slender, a wonder they took the strain.

Later I learned she was the American Girl
'at Naragansett Park, Providence in June 1869,
winning from Miss Lucy Palmer and Lady Thorn'.
The print from a mansion-house sale, no level
terrain beyond Tarbolton but a limbo I could
only imagine. Until a glimpse of the rural
mid-West beyond Cleveland Heights, past
wealthy domains with their own polo grounds,

brought the trotting American Girl to mind.
Soil bleached, hedgerows plumed, I now see
my great-uncle in his element, coursing as never
before; spokes whirring, wheels puffing
up dust-clouds, jockey-cap silky with light:
a timely resurrection (regardless of his theology)
amidst spacious vistas – Old Glory streaming,
and yellow ribbons, tied round each oak tree.

II

Jawbone Walk

'It must have been all underwater
once. You're welcome to share my bench.
Where was I? Yes, a time when the entire

Meadows roared with the surge of seas.
Could you spare something towards lunch?
Thank you, sir. Yes, rather than trees

soughing, translucent waves rampaging. How else
do you imagine that arch got there? The ocean
has *haves* and *have-nots* too, you know, though

you might not think it. Never hear
of the scavenger crab? Don't suppose you
give it a thought. Must've been millions

of years before the Brontosauruses
came huffing this way, far less the Legions
who tramped north, only to disappear.

Much appreciated miss, no need to scurry away…
In the Pleistocene Age or thereabouts,
it must have been. Excuse me sir, have you the price

of a cup of tea? That's rich, I must say –
you wouldn't like to add a sandwich? Yes,
those jaw-bones have been around a long time.'

As he pockets my sub, and keen to remain
a one-off do-gooder, not form a habit,
I ask can we treat it as a season ticket.

Past bedraggled Sunday footballers,
kite-fliers and frisbee-throwers,
dogs single-mindedly at their business,

he heads down Middle Meadow Walk towards
the Infirmary outbuildings:
yellow-eyed, looming Mastodons.

Inheritance

When first we came to this city
there were nights we would lie
too tense to sleep for fear
the noises we could hear,

muffled blows, a woman's screams,
stemmed from real violence.
So it proved. In the small hours
she rang our bell, in her nightdress,

weals on her face, to use the phone.
One morning to our relief, they'd gone.
More pleasing sounds, if rarer silences,
now infiltrate our living space.

For all that, this a land ill at ease
with itself. Brutality decrees
its own choreography: small children
fastened at the wrist by coloured ribbon;

pavements laden with flowers
in cellophane. The fascination
of lens and screen forcing us
to choose, or not, to be voyeurs.

Short, from tempering justice
to compounding bestiality.
As deep, fear of being rendered,
through familiarity, immune to horror.

So are we at the mercy of the world we live in,
yet blessed as to some: one's son on heroin;
another traced to London, not heard of again.
The test, more and more, just to endure.

If so, what the likely adequacy
of our strain? Dawn comes. Reluctantly
I open the shutters, turn the radio on.
Scientists have found a link in human evolution:

a fossilised skeleton, adding to our ancestry
a further million years. What family-tree
can compete with primordial gloom, the cave-man
in you croaks sagely, to the cave-man in me.

Previous Occupants

Of the previous occupants they will ask drily,
can you explain the internal division, and why
the rooms are appointed that curious way?

As for the decor, all one can say
is it renders one speechless. These colours
are *yours*? And *that's* what you'd have us pay!

So I imagine our successors viewing offhandedly
where we lived contentedly, down the years.
Rather than succumb to time's passage, let us

with what's left, muzzle terror in happiness.
As life goes on, we learn to pay its toll.
Walls that protect, can also hem us in. All

in degree: as next door's sycamore
gave shelter, but had to be cut down
for blocking out the light. Our cherry even,

in some great gale, might smash a window in.
Hard too, to concede these days are gone
when our bodies did all required of them:

our grown sons a reminder of energies passed on,
as in their exploits on acreages of green
they put bat to ball or striding for the line

launch into the tackle with scant concern;
gaze fixed, unflinchingly, on far
horizons... their predestined future.

At the Reservoir

As I skirt Thriepmuir a car door opens
and a voice asks where I'm heading. The water's
edge seemingly a farm boundary, I prepare
to retrace my steps – but garb and demeanour
flouting no convention, am permitted to walk on.

A quaffing at a pure source: geese ready
to head north; permutations of umber
and green. So that when a moorhen scutters
from under my feet, and a bunting in mufti
nose-dives into a reed-bed and sways there

like a vaulter on a pole, I contain
a spontaneous chortle: just not done,
to distract attention from the mundane
business of householder and family-man
or old age, our fast-approaching destination.

Three Ages of Man

(c. 1510-15)

Titian certainly had it going for him:
a hirsute herdsman with a Tuscan tan,
a skimpy cloth over his loins; against
umbrous boscage, one arm round a country lass,
garlanded and in a low-cut summer dress,
unabashed by his near-nakedness.
Two recorders aspirate their happiness
as vibrant with life and love's maturity
they gaze at each other lingeringly;
while opposite post-prandially slumber
a pair of infants, all crinkly innocence
yet lovers in embryo, guarded over
by a winged amorino. In the mid-distance
reclines a white-bearded, bald old man,
a skull in each hand to underline
time's undermining, unerringly to come.

Hard to credit this Arcady casually
encountered, so entrancing its pastorality.
The danger, that such composed harmonies
should, beyond delighting the eye,
enhance notions of noble savagery.
Transposed to our century certainly,
juxtaposings of Childhood, Maturity
and Age would present increasingly
images of War's ravages, Man's lust:
from those sacrificed in the Holocaust,
to latter-day 'ethnic cleansings'
and martyrdoms; countenanced cruelty;
presented in any equivalent tableau,
children starving in desert or ghetto;
in what passes as peace, parents laid low
by virus, grandparents through dementia...

But War aside, back in the 16th century,
reduction by enfeeblement and disease:
Titian's own late portraits a witness,
decades after the death of Giorgioni
from Plague, to human pain and fallibility.
This an early instance of his response
to physical love – and its transience;
his grasp on brush and palette knife,
countering thoughts of grief and strife,
matched by the firmness of his hold on life;
what he achieves so wondrously,
the illusion of time frozen, sadly
a function not of our lives lived daily,
but of his benignity and spirituality:
through Art, dignity not negated
by loss, but dread of death abated.

As we pass the National Gallery's
smooth pillars, his masterpiece occupies
my mind's eye – as earlier it appeared
on the streaming pane of a hospital ward,
a liquescence of colour, hallucinatory
almost, and only fleetingly transposed
with what took painful precedence:
in our presence, a mind discomposed,
frailty yearning for tranquillity,
oblivious of the bustling capital
we have escaped to; by an irony,
the building doubly a *memento mori*,
one red-brick wall retaining
as a relic of medieval days the name
Saint Roque, patron of sufferers; haven,
then burial ground, for Plague victims.

Losing Touch

I *Visit*

Today on arrival, we sense a further
adaptation to environment: limited
movement, in a darkening habitat;
dulling of response to muted stimulus –

suggesting for all the world some blurred
figure underwater, its sole motion the slow
undulation of its tail, the quiver of a fin;
no more than needed, to shift position.

Conversation flows sluggishly, apart from
sparks of animation, till it's time
to go. Our departure arouses an agitation
as though relating to something undone.

Seeing us wave from the driveway below
she moves an arm, as if tugging aside
a non-existent curtain: the impression
as of fronds clearing, a reassertion

of old perspectives, the loss of dignity
entailed; her window the wall of an aquarium
hemming her in. With no warning,
a pang of pain spans the space between.

II *Losing touch*

I feel so confused. If only
I could sleep peacefully away.
We are living far too long nowadays.
Still, ninety is a good age, you agree?

Like a mantra, over and over,
between journeyings to far-off
resorts; exotic countries
and residences, vicariously

visited down the years;
now subterfuge experiences.
I envisage her fears
as so many furred moths

in a ferment between her
and the light; a journey
through a trance-like forest,
the abyss so close...

day-to-day life an instrument
she has all but forgotten
how to play – so long in a dusty
loft, its strings slack anyway.

III *Ghosts*

Driving home for Sunday tea, we used
to pass along the highways and byways
of her girlhood, while she reminisced
about school and university days;

pointing out where she caught
the Dalkeith bus, when she taught;
then on our return, Gladstone
Terrace where she was born.

Recalling her graduation ceremony
in the McEwan Hall, the principal's
felicitous 'It seems no one, Mr Liddell,
can pass you, but for the examiners...'.

Hard not to suspect, afterwards,
I was inheriting her ghosts:
the Meadows swirling with mist,
frilled shapes under the trees

and right where she said they were,
to no skirl of pipes and drums
or male voices in full song,
the Dandy Ninth, going off to War.

IV *Reiteration*

I seem hopelessly lost.
Worse than ever. I used
to be in a halfway house.
Nothing approaching this…

Hardly a stone's throw
from the window, snow
powders Blackford Hill
where she played as a girl.

Little more merciless
than the ageing process:
ice filling the veins;
a hawk's glinting talons.

Her wrist frail on mine
I think despairingly of Man
and his Creator, exploding
from the Sistine ceiling;

yet when helplessly
she beseeches to be gone,
find I can pray only
that her will be done.

V *Oratorio*

She has shown no response
to Holy Week, as in earlier
days and down the years.
Nor do the signatures

on the Easter cards heaped
by her bedside convey other
than that they too relate
to an impenetrable past.

Bach at his most sublime
depicts Death, seen
through Satan vanquished
and Christ risen, as no more

than a gentle slumber
prior to entering Heaven.
The vision of her bowed
head, nodding slowly,

accentuates the mortality
invested in that fragile
frame. The chorus nears
its end. Jubilant voices soar.

Strathclyde Concerto
No.8 for bassoon

First an eye-glance, that tryst
between conductor and soloist,
to enhance our expectancy:
then a maiden voyage under way.

Glintings of ancient piracies
mingle with homelier harmonies
as she charts unfamiliar seas,
part clipper, part man-o'-war:

glissando liquescences,
the cellos' mellow buoyancies;
spume-flurry of flute and bassoon;
pizzicato forays, as reefs beckon.

Sensing hidden profundities,
mysteries rewarding mastery,
we respond simply and joyously
to mirrorings and melodies

whose entrancement mesmerises,
until the composer – no longer
agitato – deftly steers us
through the shallows to harbour.

An instant's giddy stillness.
Then as he turns and bows
the prow dips to applause:
an aural splicing of the mainbrace!

Surfaces

A pottery lamp-base bought, you ask for another.
And weeks later, find she forgot to note the order.
You point out one as right but for the colour,
its blue unsuited to your room's intended decor.
The glazes identical, it's a question of thickness,
she explains; all she can do (if she remembers)
is try to keep it thin, so the companion-piece
(with luck) is close to the sea-sheen you're after.

Your skin has a glow, from your recent holiday;
a warmth of fleshtone you haven't borne for ages;
more than a response merely to the sun's rays,
or arbitrary firing of a surface glaze.
My mind turns to the dazzle of breaking waves
like those in your photos from Pacific caves
which thrill with the brightnesses they show,
while a reminder of irresistible forces below.

Globe Trotter

(for Sue Meek)

Before setting out she weighed carefully
whether to travel with the sun or against,
which airlines to avoid, the itinerary
most likely to elude the world's angst.

In the event she took like a duck to water
in steaming Boston, San Francisco's penumbra,
among the National Park's giant sequoias
or literally in the hot springs of Rotorua,

Fijian rain-forest. Home again, all blurs.
Till heavy with sleep, she remembers
out of the blue the Chinese fortune-teller
who scrutinising her outstretched palm

informed her she had financial worries
at work, then predicted she'd marry
at thirty-eight and bear two children
to a man who would not talk to her.

Only time will tell. May her horizons
meanwhile remain happily unconstrained –
but without precluding Fortune's
often inscrutable manifestations.

Sainte Foy

In the Cathedral at Conques, under a glass case,
we confront the life-sized reliquary of Ste Foy:
of beaten gold, containing the bones of a child;
studded over the years, with gems and intaglios
from the faithful. The eyes aquamarine. Unable
to equate girlish vivacity with so icy an effigy,
such extravagance with sanctity, I leave the chamber
with its powdery light, return to the outside air.

Hard enough for God's sake, immaculately to retain
images of a loved one, memories of when he or she
was here. Yet others will readily tell you to put on
a brave face, to show you've come to terms with pain;
so that you construct around yourself a carapace
they regard as normal; whatever poise you retain
reassuring for those who assume banked embers
are extinct – not guessing they still may blaze.

Presence

(i.m. D.K.)

Each time I come fishing here now brings me past
where you hit what fate had brought the other way.
Tonight, the April light fading, the ripples flatly

slapping the bow assume an added melancholy. But as
the dazzling intricacies of even a minute ago
give way to darkness, and the hills enclosing us

become undulations of velvet (as Border hills do),
so in a manner no less real because wondrous
you seem both present, and absent, in the afterglow.

White-out

Blindingly from the east, blizzards come.
    The first flakes sizzle on the stove,
as the storm gathers momentum.
    Were we in such a land, my love...

It is of you we think, children of Bosnia,
    your ghosts like white birds passing
over, passing over: so that already
    the sky is black with your wings.

Above the Storm

'At altitude, conditions will worsen.' Inevitably
the first snow comes at the top of the gully,
as I unzip my anorak and pour a mug of tea.
Sod's law; and Nature's too. As in real
life, things deteriorate when we least want it.

At this moment though, I'm assured your flight
will be above the storm (worst for 25 years
the weatherman said) as you head for Los Angeles,
then Auckland. I hope they're right, and that
your long-awaited trip gets off to a smooth start.

*

At some point during a storm-tossed night
I peer at the faintly luminous face
by my bed, try to calculate
where you might be. At eight-thirty
in the evening, you could well be out

for that dinner with Angela and George:
a gathering too discreet to gorge
yourselves American-style, but capable
I'm sure of eating well. Sleep calls.
Bon appetit! I'll let you pay the bill.

*

Two midnights later. You will have flown
(if on schedule) over Hawaii, and soon
be crossing the International date-line:
short-cutting from yesterday to tomorrow.
As I stand at your plant-strewn kitchen window

my heart tells me there should be some sign
visible at least over your own tended garden.
No shooting-star – did I really expect one –
but in the gap between the tenements opposite,
the sky is decked with garlands of pure white.

*

If on time, you will be touching down
on the other side of the globe; whilst I
have sat virtually stationary, over poetry
about and to you. The one intervention,
visiting my mother, who remembered you'd gone.

In the early Twenties, she spent a holiday
in France, her furthest ever from home.
But when I mention New Zealand, she says some
of her happiest memories are of Dunedin:
'so long ago... I can't recall with whom.'

*

Will our times in the Hautes Alpes and Provence
stick in the memory, bright transparencies?
Or as the decades pass, comprise
some previous lost existence,
merging with more mundane scenes,

all transposed; or be replaced entirely
by phantom tours and cruises
in the fuddled mind? If so, will they
by joyous or sad? And are we likely
both to inhabit them – or each, separately?

*

Sunday. I wonder if you're worshipping
in the same neat church I sat in, when
so briefly there. Nothing Victorian,
but stripped pine, with modern carving.
A well-behaved New Plymouth congregation

sang rousingly, then gave the lengthy sermon
full attention – never wavering
(that I could see) as a line of ants came in
one window, skirted the organ screen
and on reaching the far wall, disappeared.

*

Since it is mellow afternoon with you,
treat this short section as a *billet doux*.
I picture you anchored in a bay of blue
where you enjoy, with John and Liffey,
a swim in water (why not the old cliché)

still crystal-clear. Laughter reaches me,
like tinkling bells. From the boat's side
come lappings of applause, as if on cue.
I send my love as, colourfully clad,
carefree you set, then light, your barbecue.

*

Again I visit my mother. Her room brims
with the fragrance of unseasonal roses.
She sits as though tranced, in prisms
of light and shade. 'Is it time to go down?'
The blooms tremble, in their fluted vase.

A pair of gulls, swooping past, are mirrored
in the glass of a photo. An inner voice
similarly reduces her presence, and mine,
to no more than a fleeting reflection
of Life outside: a moment, then gone...

*

Your papyrus plant, which I was to water
on alternate days, forgotten utterly.
The extent of my neglect: its slender
stems are bowed; dried leaftips shrivel;
its elegant parasols, all forlorn.

For such mishaps, desperate remedies. I pour
bottlefuls in, night and morning. No sign
of recovery. Too late the familiar, bitter
lesson: little use a surfeit of affection,
once the initial damage has been done.

*

This where we used to walk with the boys,
when they were young; along this track,
past the reservoir. I sense their absence
and our replacement, by new generations.
If only I'd had the wisdom then I imagine

I have now, how simple it would have been
to resolve this, or that; which course
to choose, which not. Next time remember,
in life as with water divining: seize
the wand firmly – but with receptive wrist.

*

Meanwhile the crystal ball darkens;
so much of what they should inherit
polluted, or going up in flames;
storm-clouds on every horizon. Nowhere
Man cannot render unfit for habitation.

Nor closeness to home an assurance
of sanctuary. Our lives shadowed
by hatred and intolerance,
each massacre of the innocents shows
we can kill our saints, before they're born.

*

When you left you took with you a tiny Tiki,
traditionally to keep evil spirits away
and no doubt as good an amulet as any.
All I can do, when again you fly
around the world, is wish you godspeed

without trusting it to ward off danger
any more than a St Christopher medal did
before his downgrading, or for that matter
the grey-bearded patriarch we were taught
presided over us, in childhood.

*

Your spirit meantime flits about the place,
from those items bought in auctions
in our early days, to the cushions
scattered in the sitting-room, the rummers
and yellow plates displayed downstairs;

elsewhere the angling of a lampshade,
consistent with where the pictures
look their best. And latest of all,
your newly-lined bedspread: untenanted
it keenly awaits you, discreetly autumnal.

*

And see, against the net curtains
like a screen print: the papyrus
in its brass bowl. Assiduously
cared for since my sin of ommission,
it has recovered miraculously –

conjuring up visions of Nefertiti,
Thales proclaiming *water is all*;
the rushes Moses was left in,
by the Nile. Yet how convince
you I've hand-maidened it well?

*

What about: only yesterday I cut
its largest leaves into strips;
the pith beaten, and rolled
with mud substitute; then pressed
under the mattress on wooden slats

with fitting devotions, to produce
the flimsy parchment this is written on.
Forgive its clumsy hieroglyphs. Even
if you don't believe a word of them,
the important thing is: welcome home.

III

McGonagall's Map Reconnoitring

Scratch a shard of Iberian monchiquite, you could.uncover
Caithness cadences; in the Tasman acetate you crouch over,

a Border lilt. Peruvian littoral-filterings may reveal
Hebridean vocables – or honest-to-God Glaswegian gutturals.

Scotland over the years through its pioneers and explorers
(greater and lesser) has been an avid exporter of nomenclatures:

from Canada's Mackenzie River and the Victoria Falls
to crescents and terraces inspired by the *Waverley* novels;

place-names round the globe (Perth, Glencoe, Dunedin…)
cogent witnesses to a pattern of diaspora and migration.

But despite the vastness of the atlas with which to juggle
there is, so far as I can determine, just one Auchenshuggle.

French Connection

(in celebration of the Auld Alliance, 1295-1995)

What amalgam of nationhood and sentimentality
induces in us Scots such lachrymosity?

When in the bluster and skite of Hogmanay,
smooth as an oyster in stout, the old year slips away;

or bagpipes skirling and glengarries doffed,
the haggis's reeking entrails are raised aloft.

Grown men are known to weep in caravanserai
by yon Bonnie Banks, or crossing the sea to Skye;

while comics (Glesca and other) employ their wiles
to reduce us to crumpled Kleenex, in the aisles.

A more solemn lump comes to the throat at losses
on foreign fields, those rows of receding crosses;

or posthumously honouring men of girth
driven by inner demons to the ends of the earth

on feet of clay: remote anniversaries
an enticing diversion from today's injustices.

Given that accident of birth and blood decree
which flag has first call on our loyalty

have these seven centuries of Auld Alliance
borne fruit, or merely fuelled defiance

of the common enemy happed in imperial power,
its emblems the village green, the Bloody Tower;

alternate bombast and disparagement
occupying the vacuum of self-government?

Somehow we manage to survive such rancour
(English paradoxically, our *lingua franca*);

increasingly employing on sporting occasions
the vocabulary of war, to stoke our passions:

viz football's lunacy – or the true romance
of Big Gavin's glorious try at Parc des Princes,

manly metaphor for entente between Nations,
or separatist's excuse for more libations.

Words to a rousing tune can cause a riot,
albeit so spurious the head won't buy it.

Though often riven by ambivalence
the heart knows no dilemma in this instance:

O Flower of Scotland quickly mists my gaze,
but my pulse races to the *Marseillaise*.

Norman Collie at Sligachan Inn

Collie is still up in Skye like an eagle in his eyrie but I hope he will get tired of that lonely vigil and come back to London.

Ropes and ice-axes stashed, the climbers
troop into the dining-room, nodding towards
the fine-featured octogenarian who slowly
sips his wine. Puffing his pipe afterwards

in the corrugated-iron smoking-room, eyes
like quartz chips, he gives nothing away
at their expressions of amazement that
so many peaks thought previously unclimbed

should be capped by such similar cairns.
He smiles as they plan the next day's
routes and traverses; recalling his own
and Mackenzie's mastery of the Bhasteir Tooth,

solving the massive shadow of the Cioch...
They say goodnight, oblivious of his
unspoken benediction: 'Set your sights
on your aspirations' limit. The summit won,

let the eye gaze, the spirit brim. Then
the gods of the mountain not taking kindly
to abuse of hospitality, make your way down,
recharged and calm. Nearing the treeline

you will encounter colours intense as any
you recall, cow-bells resonant in the inner ear.
Gaze back at the crest where you've been,
its blueness nothing on its own – rather

the use you put it to.' Continents merge
as he drifts towards sleep, pursued by troupes
of Edwardian ladies, ropes round hourglass waists,
who slip from precipices, abseil into the abyss.

Later he turns in a cold sweat: Mummery
and Whymper, as on a glass plate, spin past
in a neon blaze; voices in whispers ask,
was the rope frayed or mysteriously cut?

Until eased by a chuckle, at his request
that Leverhulme sponsor an attempt on Everest:
in return, they'd plant a flag on the summit,
a bar of Sunlight Soap emblazoned on it.

Air and Water

(for James Rankin)

The Bible beaten into him (thrashed excessively
but exclusively on week-days, to preserve the calm
of the Sabbath) Muir one of three children (the others
left with their mother in Dunbar) taken to settle
in the Winsconsin prairie. First Fountain Lake;

then Hickory Hill where when he was twelve his father,
desperate to hit water, lowered him in a bucket
with hammer and chisel, to hack obdurate sandstone out.
Eighty feet down, the air so carbonised he collapsed
and could have died, if not hauled to the surface.

Subsequently University, and departure from home:
thereafter his own man. But nightmares the remainder
of his life, choking in an underground pit – the father
stentorian as ever; his comeuppance that his son,
Nature's disciple, would not credit its glories to God.

Years later on the Yosemite trail, the thrawn
old Scotchman he'd become leaping naked from a snow-pool
to challenge his President to a wrestling-bout:
an immigrant, battling for his American dream,
tackling Big Business head-on. The marvel, he won.

Roosevelt, needing the Californian vote, later
to welch on him, turning Hetch-Hetchy into a dam.
Muir still worshipping his open spaces, the supreme
escape from that father who drove him below ground.
What better than a Wilderness, to liberate the mind.

Camp Jedibe

Slitted against unsteady candlelight
the eyes opposite, for all their laughter-lines,
have been near death. We've been told that.

A wild-life photographer researching a book
he was charged by an old Kruger bull
and trampled unconscious, ribs broken,

a hip dislocated, skin scoured from face
and arms by the bristled foreleg he clung to;
saved somehow from the tusks' *coup de grâce.*

He converses fluently, in measured tones;
listens well. Shows no hint of machismo.
He doesn't need to. He is the real thing.

Early next morning we spin for barbel
in the lagoon, thousands of dollars worth
of Nikon equipment trained on us. What

a moment to land one. Not to be. The rest
of the aquatic world wakens. Mosquitos
home in. A crocodile surfaces near our stern.

That night under a hissing paraffin-lamp
we learn that what gnaws at him is why,
having him in its power, the elephant

let him live. Beyond this (real
measure of the man) how it is likely
to react when it next senses his smell.

Upper Clyde

Upstream

Clydes Burn, Daer, Potrail,
   true source in dispute;
Elvan, Midlock, Wandel
   adding their tribute.

Forces thus joined,
   we'll stick together
all the year round,
   best and worst of weather.

Over sand and gravel,
   skirting mill and quarry,
for us it's downhill
   all the way to the sea.

First light

Near Nunnerie, where Daer and Potrail meet,
highstepping it through early morning mist:
a troupe of llamas; one brown, four white,
their heads-erect posture midway between
goat and camel, last thing we dreamt we'd see.

Approaching the bank, they stop in unison
and stand motionless, maybe in contemplation
of their near perfect reflections, or simply
for a good nostrilful of us, then move on;
all but the largest, who gazes quizzically

as if asking, 'Do you fear we don't exist,
other than as some mutation of the spirit
of the place? Have it as you please'.
Dismissing such philosophical fripperies
he turns and splashes through a hoop of light.

Voices

These rounded-up Kirkhope shearlings,
impervious to our amateur tup-glowering,
are dipped a warm caramel brown
so their black and white faces are best shown.

Drawn to Lanark Sale next day
we relish the voices round us, variations
within constancies of accent and speech-pattern
rich as clotted cream: as such jealously

to be guarded, not derided by some jejune
education secretary or other pedant;
any undermining of tradition
and identity, part of a wider impoverishment.

War memorial

She lives not far from the war memorial.
Two boys, running past, kicking a ball,
spark off memories; how going to school

her brother hid his boots for fear
his classmates would resent a wealth not theirs
and punch it out of him. And how years

later his diary became hers,
as next of kin; among its entries,
'One sign things are getting serious,

platoon football put under lock and key';
and *'Today found my boots missing, lucky*
to obtain another pair, in the vicinity.'

Between, the telegram; the realisation
it was all over; that they'd never again
cartwheel in the spray of Corra Lynn.

Orchard country

Far from French groves, all gnarl and sun-glow,
Crossford's clay haughs nonetheless thrive;
swagged branches bearing not grape or olive
but a more northerly fruit, whose bloom no one
expects will *take the light* like a model's skin.

Abundance lessening, still set in due season
not under the azures of the Glasgow Boys'
southern travels, but the no-nonsense skies
they left and returned to: whites and greys
in gurly cloud-clusters, unkempt tresses.

Contrasts

A reverberant monument to pomposity and pride,
Hamilton Mausoleum housed the sarcophagus
El Magnifico bought as his last resting-place:
despite chiselling Egyptian basalt out,
for his insertion, sledge-hammers needed.

On the skyline the pink pavilion-towers
of Chatelherault, the ducal *Dogg Kennells*;
Adam's charred interiors ornately restored,
the formal parterre and Cadzow cattle
heightening the impression of a film set.

After such lavishness, leave the main road
at a sign (easy to miss) pointing the way
to a small church, loft and spire unfussy,
a single row of weavers' cottages opposite;
and the Dalserf ferry long-since obsolete,

sit as though marooned, history's shadows
sifting and lengthening, looked down on
by an obelisk to '*the Rev. John McMillan,
Covenanter of Covenanters*'; an 11th century
hogback grave-stone adding its *memento mori*.

From the air

Brochures offer trips, no effort spared,
by Hot Air Balloon, over the Clyde Valley;
sustaining basketry, the roar generated,
enabling you to look down on the vastly
variegated patchwork below, and see
glinting in watery sunlight the glasshouses
of a dwindling economy, orchards under
threat; beyond, the unprettified mass
of derelict steelworks, abandoned pits,
alongside the scars of opencast; and wonder
as the remnants queue up for benefit
or redundancy, or cough fluid from lungs
rotted by silicosis, how soon fibreglass
shafts and slagheaps will emerge complete
with a reconstructed workforce of miners
and smelters, once backbone and sinew
of this Central Belt. The last straw
in usurping sacrifice: some future balloon
expending its hot air over a giant *Lanark
Industrial Disney-Land and Theme Park.*

Envoi

Howking out rocks for a new generator,
an earthmover muddies the flow at Blantyre weir:
alongside, a fish-ladder. Its course cleared,
will the damage outweigh benefit to Nature
or salmon reappear, thrusting upriver
where none was seen for sixty years or more?

A stroll away, the ruins of Bothwell Castle
on its greensward peninsula, walls
coalescing in sunshine with the browns
and russets of autumn beeches, demolition
and reconstruction a test of fortitude;
its donjon a bulwark to the Upper Clyde.

Body Language

In the courtyard of the Metropolitan
Museum this sizzling forenoon
a couple dance, inseparable
as any pair could be. Baseball-

capped, not like Astaire
but with a stevedore's shoulders,
he bucks and whirls his partner,
her skirt a blur of colour.

But the dispersal of fine spray
as they shimmy past is his only:
not just cheek to cheek, this gigolo
and his danseuse are stitched toe to toe;

no flesh and blood but a lifesize doll,
her exuberance a *trompe l'œil*
make-believe. Galatea and Pygmalion,
translated to the heart of Manhattan.

Te Maori

Plane-loads of numbered wooden crates
delivered to the Metropolitan Museum
for the *Te Maori* Exhibition, a run
of near-disasters is ascribed to those
whose spirits they contain signalling anger
at being regarded as mere *objets d'art*.

After discussion behind the scenes,
the opening ceremony goes smoothly.
Then the discovery of severe notching
in a jade head coincides with dispute
over an extension of dates: the matter
resolved, damage no longer seen.

Where, given our ingrained materialism –
the absence of green-stone carvings
on our lawns, combs cut from bone –
might the spirits of our ancestors
reside? Up to us, to preserve
our own repositories of intuition.

Past Glories

Grappling most days with verbal
doodles and pen-pictures, I take a stroll
on occasional afternoons, to refuel

the batteries. The National Portrait Gallery
is not just a collection of paintings, more
a cross between time-capsule and reliquary.

Today I study two boys, their golfing gear
a designer potpourri, a garish reminder
that eighteenth century tartanry bore

little relation to clan or family. Opposite,
a proud retainer pipes his heart out
in front of Castle Grant, both wings complete

and symmetrical, a projection
of the laird's impecunious imagination
never built. Out again in slanting rain,

the moral's clear. Beware of too naively
swallowing the fruit on every family tree –
or hoping delusions of grandeur will fool posterity.

This is not to be dismissive of past glories:
let an awareness of them contribute rather
to a refining, and defining, of what you really are.

Choosing a Drawing

(for Ronald Rae)

'I keep several hundred in a friend's attic,
some so depressing you couldn't face
living with them. Your best tactic

is to avoid preconceptions, then choose
whatever speaks most strongly to you.'
In charcoal whorls, an elephant and hippo,

baggy bulk conveyed by gradations of light
and shade; portfolios on biblical themes;
a series of Grassmarket down-and-outs

drawn long before this became the fashion –
ghosted features left to the imagination.
At last I choose essence of sheep. Head down,

grey streaks scoring the flanks, a pink blur
across its back the only presence of colour,
it captures the ambivalence of nature:

one moment a celebratory leap into spring air;
the next, world's weight, down-tug of gravity.
At the mercy of irreconcilables, I marvel

how in pen and ink or granite, he can impose
such order; through controlled frenzy, convey
the terror, and tenderness, of his inner eye.

Boudin at the Burrell

Astonishing how his blurry clusters of promenaders
with parasols, washerwomen and shrimpers
wading in the shallows, should be so varied;
especially when rather than venture out to sea
he kept returning to beach and jetty, at low tide.

Dreamer and loner, throughout his life he happily
narrowed his horizons, enabling us to drink in
those elements he made his own. The secret,
his gift for capturing cloud formations, fine
or bearing rain; their silky turbulence.

Contemplating those bathing-boxes drawn by horses
he was never the voyeur, detesting Trouville's summer
masquerade of gilded parasites and poseurs. Nor fond
of distances: as lengthy a journey as any when he died
and was transported to be alongside his wife, in Montmartre.

Search

Several sightings: alone or with her daughter
who vanished with her. Such distances

impossible in the time, all dismissed as figments
of the imagination. Until shreds of dress

seen snagged on thorn, some with stains on them.
Such occurrences more and more frequent; searches

revealing little. Nor are real Muses readily found.
Yet every so often the blood will leap to a shimmer

as of white chiffon at the periphery
of seeing: a lost fragment, drifting in the mind.

Fauve

Familiar motifs: ornamental
animals clashing; patterned cattle

on russet hillsides; over the fireplace,
a concerto of barbaric harmonies.

Upstairs, garish prints of tigers,
a gouache of a man on a dromedary,

decorative floribunda. But by far
the most predatory creature there

the girl who runs the gallery:
night eyes; rhinestone rings

on splayed talons; tawny
hair aslant, like a hawk's wing.

In Your Dreams

(for James Aitchison)

Choosing between Jung and Freud
revealed, I was told, the kind
of father I'd have preferred.
My affinity, I confess, ever
with the twinkling eyed one:
so much that he preoccupied
my waking thoughts for years
(only he could vouch for hours
of sleep). Later I encountered
another from the same mould:
Konrad Lorenz, more mellow
than rigid rules would allow –
and so transposed them
that one night I came across
the analyst up to his waist
in a smooth-flowing stream,
hotly pursued by patients
in the guise of greylag geese.

Strangers in the Night

A fallen angel probably lurks within us all.
JACK VETTRIANO

Ways of dealing with dreams vary.
We used to act complicitously –

Nightmare Creatures, caught slithering
across the sill, susceptible to taming;

Wild Things which once overcome
enabled you to settle down

in an unmenaced cot, in the belief
they helped you prepare for later life.

Now press a button, you despatch your enemies;
Fact or Fiction, simply blow them away.

Adult desire and guilt conversely
have a knack of gnawing remorselessly

as when aroused by the caress
and thrill of these canvases,

scenes of dubious comings and goings,
mesmerising liaisons,

liquescent silk, nocturnal satin,
louche entrée to the imagination –

till at the portals of the gallery,
deciphering a spidery '*mysteriously*

troubling and melancholic'
in the well-thumbed visitors' book

you thrust your way outside
for fear you can no longer hide

that give-away glint in your eye,
or keep Monsters within at bay.

Lady Anne's Diary

I *On her arrival*

'Our messmates numbered about twenty-four, and we all got on like lambs...'

Our party despatched, a sickly
old viceroy's ears and eyes;
chess-pieces for Henry Dundas.

A disparate cargo:
the crew and ourselves,
a shipment of gun barrels for Bengal.

Mercifully hitting it off. Not least
John Barrow, man of infinite maps and charts
intent on mastering the Interior

(through whose inducement
I'd clamber up Table Mountain,
himself happily wedding a girl from the Cape).

To signal our approach, flags hoisted
and cannon-fire, smoke-puffs
dispersing over what had been

for eight long days on our horizon.
One summit a lion *couchant*, briefly
as though in the lea of Arthur's Seat.

A prime aim, to discover 'how far the same
objects may appear alike in British
and Dutch eyes'; construe the difference.

II *In the Cape*

Soon established, besides the rat-tat
familiar through haar from the Castle:
on buffalo hide, an ominous pulsebeat.

Ingrained, to make the Dutch good Englishmen:
myself unprepared for such dominance –
some up to seven feet, hefty for a minuet.

(Later I recited Auld Robin Grey,
as they sat morosely
in their blue cloth jackets, incongruous top-hats.)

In return, countenanced with a fixed smile
feasts of aromatic nastiness; trestles
boasting calf's head, horns boiled and all.

Urged to avoid religion and politics
even among ourselves (certain clerical goings-on
irksome to my father-in-law, Bishop of Limerick).

The Peninsula an objective, not as a vessel
of milk and honey, vineyards and gleaming gables,
but a slender sentinel to India.

As for the wilderness beyond, savagery
and worse. Constant whetting of War's cutlery.
To secure this gateway, I fear many will die.

III *Lady Anne's Insomnia*

Reiterated, as time went on: 'the best thing
for these Dutch, to take the oath of allegiance,
who certainly will not see their flag fly again'.

Nor clandestine, but trilled by Macartney
and his Generals at the tops of their voices:
no need to intercept communiques, letters home.

(My own origin conveniently forgotten,
the injunction to quell 'the unruly Scots'
indecorously bellowed in King George's anthem.)

Most onerous, keeping the peace: not between
tribal factions, but one Officer
and another, out to make a reputation;

resorting minimally to sleight of hand,
whether in Love or War. The winners,
consistently those who hold their liquor.

These evenings see us playing croquet
on the residency lawns; so still the air
the gum-trees decked with candles, like chandeliers.

My husband up-country I lie awake
in the small hours counting gourds clicking
through hoops, kissing like heads in a basket.

NOTES

Kilmarnock Edition *(page 11)*: The first edition of *Poems, Chiefly in the Scottish Dialect* by Robert Burns, 1786.

Norman Collie at Sligachan Inn *(pages 60-61)*: Collie (1859-1942), mountain climber and pioneer, who as a biochemist discovered the properties of neon. A.F. Mummery died on Nanga Parbat, and controversy followed the loss of four of Edward Whymper's party on the Matterhorn. The prefatory quote is from *Norman Collie: a life in two worlds* by Christine Mill (AUP, 1987).

Air and Water *(page 62)*: John Muir (1838-1914) was aged eleven when his father emigrated from Dunbar, to America. He is renowned (and has belatedly been recognised in his own land) as an explorer, naturalist, author, and 'father of Conservation'. My fascination for him was rekindled through directing James Rankin's play *Yosemite*.

Contrasts *(page 66)*: Hamilton Mausoleum with its 15-second echo was built by the 10th Duke to house himself and his ancestors. The Adam hunting-lodge of Chatelherault dates from the 1730s; burnt and vandalised earlier this century, it was acquired by the nation and restored.

Te Maori *(page 69)*: The *Te Maori* (*Taonga Maori*/Treasures of the Maori) Exhibition in the early 80s launched Maori society and culture on the world. I am indebted to Carol O'Biso's remarkable account of its American tour, *First Light* (Heinemann, 1987).

Lady Anne's Diary *(pages 77-79)*: Daughter of the fifth Earl of Balcarres, Lady Anne Barnard was admired for her verve, wit and tough-mindedness in Edinburgh and at the Court of George III. She accompanied her husband to the Cape in 1797 on his appointment by Henry Dundas (later Lord Melville) as secretary to the Governor Lord Macartney.